Remodelers' Cost of Doing Business Study

2020 Edition

NAHB

National Association
of Home Builders

Remodelers' Cost of Doing Business Study, 2020 Edition

BuilderBooks, a Service of the National Association of Home Builders

Patricia Potts	Senior Director
Joel Alfaro	Cover Design
Robert Brown	Composition
Gerald M. Howard	NAHB Chief Executive Officer
Robert Dietz	Senior Vice President and Chief Economist, Economics and Housing Policy
John McGeary	Senior Vice President, Business Development and Brand Strategy
Paul Emrath	Vice President, Economics and Housing Policy
Denise Miller	Vice President, Event Product & Brand Marketing
Rose Quint	Assistant Vice President, Survey Research, Economics and Housing Policy

Disclaimer

This publication provides accurate information on the subject matter covered. The publisher is selling it with the understanding that the publisher is not providing legal, accounting, or other professional service. If you need legal advice or other expert assistance, obtain the services of a qualified professional experienced in the subject matter involved. The NAHB has used commercially reasonable efforts to ensure that the contents of this volume are complete and appear without error; however, the NAHB makes no representations or warranties regarding the accuracy and completeness of this document's contents. The NAHB specifically disclaims any implied warranties of merchantability or fitness for a particular purpose. The NAHB shall not be liable for any loss of profit or any other commercial damages, including but not limited to incidental, special, consequential or other damages. Reference herein to any specific commercial products, process, or service by trade name, trademark, manufacturer, or otherwise does not necessarily constitute or imply its endorsement, recommendation, or favored status by the NAHB. The views and opinions of the author expressed in this publication do not necessarily state or reflect those of the NAHB, and they shall not be used to advertise or endorse a product.

Published in the United States of America

23 22 21 20   2 3 4 5

ISBN-13: 978-0-86718-775-5
eISBN-13: 978-0-86718-776-2

For further information, please contact:
National Association of Home Builders
1201 15th Street, NW
Washington, DC 20005-2800
BuilderBooks.com

Contents

Figures

Tables

How to Use the Study

The *Remodelers' Cost of Doing Business Study* is conducted periodically to assess the growth, viability, and demographics of the remodeling industry. The study provides a statistically accurate analysis of remodeling businesses in terms of their size, profitability, time in the business, and number of jobs performed. It also includes multiple comparisons to previous studies. The study has a wealth of information that can be massaged to help keep score against benchmarks for today and plan for success tomorrow.

The final results include averages as well as breakdowns for the top and bottom 25% of remodelers in the study. The averages should not be considered targets or benchmarks. Rather, pay closer attention to the top 25%, as your goal is not to be just average. The report also shows results for the bottom 25% so you can see there is a range of acceptable results. Trade publications, articles by industry experts, books, and local home builders association (HBA) meetings are a few other places you can go to find performance benchmarks. Of course, the most accurate and useful benchmarks are those that reflect improvement from your own past results. This study will help you gauge your success compared with a large cross section of your peers and competitors. The study shows results based on net profit percent when defining the top and bottom 25% groups. It also includes several breakdowns by business

focus, number of jobs, and other variables to help you create a benchmark for your company.

While many of the potential benchmarks are easy to just pull off your own income statement, you shouldn't do so blindly. For example, setting goals for gross profitability is particularly dangerous unless you first understand how the study assigns various cost of goods sold or operating expenses, aka overhead. Not matching your results to the way the study assigns expenses into cost of goods sold (e.g., direct costs, above the line costs, or hard costs) will skew the margin percent radically and render your comparisons dangerous at worst or naïve at best.

The survey information was requested in a format that might be different from how you generally track your own business information and financial data. So your first order of business, (if you didn't respond to the survey and save a copy of your input) is to align your income statement with the rules of the study. Certain account totals will have to be changed to reflect a closer adherence to percent complete accounting. It is not overly complicated to slightly adjust your results to match the study, but does require you to adjust your sales, gross profit dollars, net profit dollars on the income statement and potentially either an asset account or a liability account and the net worth accounts on the balance sheet. These corrections are necessary to remove things like customer deposits or billing at given milestones, from sales for jobs on which you haven't yet earned revenue. Percent complete would also allow you to add revenue, gross profit dollars, net profit dollars and increases to an underbilling account in the assets section of the balance sheet and added Revenue, Gross profit and Net worth. This correction could be for jobs that were days from a billing milestone but it hadn't been created yet and so revenue was understated. These over billings and under billings are either subtracted or added to revenue and all the accounts that flow below that need to be changed by the same amounts. Thus if revenue falls by $10,000 because of a deposit for a job not started, $10,000 is subtracted from revenue, gross profit and net profit. That $10,000 shows up as an added liability of the same amount in the balance sheet and a reduction in the profit and loss year to date in the net worth area. Such a correction provides a more balanced look at profitability and ensures that large deposits or late billings don't skew your true year end profitability. Your accountant could do it in a flash, or it might take you 20 minutes to honestly assess which jobs you are way ahead of on billing and which you are way behind on your own.

Besides revenue timing, another area you will need to align with the study's results to make comparisons is how and where you account for field employee labor costs and benefits including taxes, insurance, pension and other expenses. The *Remodelers' Cost of Doing Business Study* survey asked respondents to pull these from overhead expense categories on their income statements and add them to a labor burden account within the cost of goods sold. Changing where you account for these costs is absolutely necessary to compare gross profit percent benchmarks, as labor burden is probably 25–80% higher than base pay for the vast

majority of contractors. Again, without these tweaks the information may lead you to believe you are kicking it, when in fact your margins may be 5–15% lower than you thought. The items that can fall into labor burden include FICA, FUTA, SUTA, workers' compensation, contractors liability, health insurance, 401K or other pension plans, tool and gas allowances, vacation, holiday, training time and expenses, sick days or other paid time off, and any other costs you care to assign. Some companies include cell phone, Internet access, computers, clothing and protective gear, and other items. For accurate comparisons, read the definitions in the study carefully so you include each item requested in the appropriate accounts.

The study is designed to rank participants' companies by their percent of net profit after deducting all expenses, including paying a reasonable salary to the owner. The two major outputs to pay attention to are net profit margin and gross profit margin (where we've included labor burden items we pulled from operating expenses, aka overhead). Make sure you include the owner's W2 pay in operating expenses before calculating net profit. Next, deduct all operating expenses from gross margin to calculate net profit.

The study addresses net profit before income taxes. Most consultants to the remodeling industry agree that viewing owner's compensation and net profit as a whole is a better way to compare any company, regardless of its legal organization (i.e., partnership, LLC, S corporation, C corporation) since the line between the owner's comp and net profits gets a little blurry. A legitimate goal for net profit is up to 10 percent, even if you don't achieve it, and 6–10% might be an appropriate target for owner's compensation. Although there is no rule of thumb, owner's compensation surely should be more than pay for your highest compensated employee by a factor of 1.2 or more, given the number of hats you wear, the risks accepted in running a business, and the usually excessive number of hours you work. Moreover, if you are not paying yourself at all or your pay is paltry, you may be raising a red flag with the IRS: your compensation cannot be less than the minimum wage.

When deciding how to react to your results compared with other companies in this study, consider that gross profit margin control is the single most important factor for success. You can control it by keeping costs of goods sold down or by raising margins relative to your competition or perceived competition. Failing to reach target volume, even with steady gross profit margins, will lead to net profit goal failure. Since volume times gross profit margin equals gross profit dollars and we can't eat margin, these two benchmarks must be watched hand in hand, both in planning and in practice, as the year goes by. Most contractors concentrate on volume without tracking trends in margin and think that working more, selling more and taking jobs (some that are not within their core competency) will lead to profit improvements. The problem with that strategy is that it fails to account for increases in overhead, field, administrative, and sales expenses that occur along with volume increases. Often, you must hire, train, and equip employees. The other issue is margin slippage, which occurs on every job, but more often and more painfully when we are busy and harried. When busy, we can ignore glitches and assumptions in our estimating systems that affect pricing strategies and project choices. In fact, the single most prevalent reason why four out of five contractors leave the business in five years is not lack of jobs but rather lack of controls and failing to react to good available financial based information.

The companies that participated in the survey are listed by how long they have been in business, so you expect those with the longest tenure to be the most profitable and have the best looking balance sheets: they are battle tested! If you are new to remodeling, pay attention to information from less experienced companies, or those with fewer employees or jobs completed, or doing volume similar to your company's. Although the study isn't statistically accurate to regions of the country, this shouldn't prevent you from ignoring some of the volume and other dollar denominated findings. But focus on the percentages, since percentages are size blind! The multiple breakdowns of number of jobs done, number of employees and years in business let you get a picture of the top/average/bottom of the market, and see how you stack up across one or more of the study outputs. Let this also be an incentive to make your own quantitative targets and spend time comparing your progress at least quarterly to track improvements.

Another area to focus on is operating expenses. The study results can help you determine if your overhead costs for sales and marketing, financing and interest, indirect expenses, and general administrative and overhead are abnormal. You can assess whether you are more efficient than the study participants at the 25th percentiles or on average. These results also can be helpful in setting realistic overall levels of spending when doing a budget for your first few years or a future year. When budgeting, remember to adjust your operating expenses for inflation, known insurance increases or additions, and other "surprises" that you can partially predict when using the study results to help with your pro-formas.

Productivity of your field and office staff is often difficult to measure, let alone reward, but the study may help you plan for future hiring as you grow volume. The study asked for the number of full-time equivalents (FTEs), of the folks who worked for their companies, broken down by function. If an employee, say the owner, spent 30% of his or her time on sales, 20% on production management, and 50% in the field, that would be equivalent to 0.3 salespeople, 0.2 production managers, and 0.5 field employees in addition to any employees that were performing those functions full time. This allows us to look at the firm's volume and divide out by the number of say field employees to see how much volume each carpenter can be expected to create. When volume is growing, the number indicates how many field employees you need to find, hire, train, and retain, or the number of trade contractors needed to produce the desired volume. The number also could indicate how much a full-time salesperson could be expected to sell. If current volume was achieved with only 0.3 full-time employees, for example, dividing current volume by 0.3 theoretically predicts how much a full-time salesperson could sell. As you plan for revenue growth, knowing how much work each type of employee can handle profitably will help you determine when you need to hire additional field employees to complete the work, more sales time or employees to sell the work, and more time for administrative and management functions.

Growth doesn't come cheap because hiring, training, and equipping new hires is expensive, and can't be ignored when this math calls for another hire. Go through the results and your own FTE facts to see how you stack up and keep this info handy for next year's budget and human resource planning.

Finally, don't let accounting frighten or confuse you. As a business owner, you must understand the important benchmarks for your business, how to continually track them during the year, and how to analyze them to spot trends that provide clues about what you need to do in pricing and cost control to make more money. This study is a great tool for starting to learn what results you should be aiming for, so use it profitably. Good luck and enjoy reading.

Alan Hanbury, Jr., CGR, CAPS, CGP, GMR, MBA

Introduction

The residential remodeling industry, just like any other private industry in the American economy, operates on the basis of competition and profits. Companies enter, stay or exit the industry of their own volition, driven by consumer demand for their services and the expectation of a rate of return commensurate with the risk taken. Because reliable information is critical to make sound business decisions, industries can help their current and potential members by producing and understanding average aggregate levels of profitability and indicators of financial health. For this reason, the National Association of Home Builders periodically conducts the *Remodelers' Cost of Doing Business Study* — a nationwide survey of residential remodeling companies designed to produce profitability benchmarks for that segment of the construction industry. The findings allow remodelers to compare their performance to that of their peers, providing cost, expense, and profit targets. Results can also highlight areas needing improvement or, in the best-case scenario, showcase a well-run, financially-solid remodeling company.

How the Study was Prepared

The 2020 *Remodelers' Cost of Doing Business Study* was conducted electronically through an online survey sent out in the spring of 2019 to about 3,700 NAHB members nationwide whose primary business activity was listed as residen-

tial remodeling. The questionnaire asked for financial and operational information, including the company's 2018 income statement and balance sheet, as well as the number of employees, number of jobs completed in different price ranges, and number of years in business. A total of 60 responses were received. Because the aim of the study is to analyze the financial performance of residential remodelers specifically, results are based solely on information from respondents who confirmed their main operation in 2018 was *residential remodeling/rehabilitation*. Not every question was answered by all respondents.

Organization of the Study

The *Remodelers' Cost of Doing Business Study, 2020 Edition* is comprised of a preamble on "How to Use the Study," followed by five chapters of study results. The study is organized as follows:

Chapters 1–3 provide detailed information on gross profits, net profits, assets, liabilities, owner's equity, and financial ratios. Chapter 1 provides this information aggregated for all residential remodelers, including a comparison between the most successful (top 25%) and least successful (bottom 25%) remodelers in terms of net profit margins. Chapters 2 and 3 present the data for general remodelers and for design-build remodelers separately.

Chapter 4 compares remodelers' performance in the South and West regions of the country (results for the Northeast and Midwest are unavailable due to low response rates from those regions) and business model (general remodeler vs. design-build remodeler). It also shows a historical comparison of gross and net profit margins going back to 1990.

Chapter 5 concludes the study providing data about the operations of survey respondents, such as the number of years in business, the number of jobs completed in different price ranges, and the number of full-time employees on payroll in 2018.

Industry Profitability

Comparing remodelers' profitability between fiscal year 2015 (the last time this study was conducted) and fiscal year 2018 shows they were successful at increasing the gross profit margin, yet higher operating expenses kept the net profit margin essentially unchanged:

- The average gross profit margin increased from 28.9% in 2015 to 30.1% in 2018.
- The average net profit margin was essentially flat, barely shifting from 5.3% to 5.2% during the same period.

Gross profit equals revenue (sales) minus the cost of sales (cost of goods sold). Cost of sales comprises:

- Labor, labor burden, materials, and trade contractors for residential remodeling/repairs
- Direct construction costs and land on secondary operations such as commercial remodeling and new single-family home building

Gross profit is measured before deducting operating expenses (indirect construction costs, financing, sales and marketing, general and administrative expenses, and owner's compensation). Here's how to calculate gross profit

as a percentage of revenue:
1. Subtract the cost of sales from total revenue.
2. Divide that gross profit by total revenue.

The following example calculates the gross profit margin for a company with $2,000,000 in total revenue and $1,400,000 in cost of sales.

$2,000,000 − $1,400,000 = $600,000 (gross profit)

$600,000 ÷ $2,000,000 = 0.30 or 30% (gross profit margin)

Net profit is the income from sales after deducting the cost of sales, as well as operating expenses and owner's compensation. In other words, net profit is the money a business earns after it has paid all the costs of both the project (hard costs) and the operating expenses (soft costs). When comparing net profits with other remodelers or with overall industry performance, it is best to consider net profits prior to tax liabilities because so many different factors can determine the amount of taxes a business pays.

Consider the same company in which total revenue is $2,000,000; cost of sales (or cost of goods sold) is $1,400,000; and operating expenses plus owner's compensation total $400,000. As mentioned earlier, the gross profit is $600,000, a gross margin of 30%. Operating expenses are 20% of revenue, and net profit is $200,000, a net margin of 10%. To calculate the net profit as a percentage of revenue, subtract the cost of sales, operating expenses, and owner's compensation from total revenue, and then divide net profit by total revenue as follows:

$2,000,000 − $1,400,000 − $400,000 = $200,000 (net profit)

$200,000 ÷ $2,000,000 = .10 or 10% (net profit margin)

1

All Residential Remodelers

Prior to this study, NAHB had conducted similar analysis on industrywide profit margins for residential remodelers in fiscal years 2003, 2011, and 2015. The latest *Remodelers' Cost of Doing Business Study* asked for financial statements for fiscal year 2018 (income statement and balance sheet), plus additional information regarding specific type of remodeling company, the number of employees on payroll, the number of jobs completed in different price ranges, and years in business. The survey questionnaire was sent electronically to about 3,700 NAHB remodeler members in April 2019. A total of 60 responses were received, but not all respondents answered every question.

Results are tabulated for all remodelers as a single group, and then broken down for those in the South and West regions of the country (the Northeast and Midwest regions had insufficient responses to produce separate reliable estimates), by type of residential remodeler, total 2018 revenue, number of jobs completed in 2018, and number of years in business. Table 1.1 shows the distribution of responses across these groups[1]. The study also analyzes results for the most and least successful group of remodelers, namely those in the top 25th percentile and bottom 25th percentile, respectively, in terms of net profit margins. The analysis is based solely on responses from members who reported their main operation to be residential remodeling/rehabilitation.

The majority — 69 percent — of remodelers participating in the study operate in two regions of the United States: 37 percent in the South and another 32 percent in the West. The remaining almost one-third of responses came from the Northeast and Midwest regions, but they are insufficient to produce reliable estimates for each one of those regions independently.

Table 1.1. Respondents' Profile	
Region	**% of total**
Northeast	16
Midwest	16
South	37
West	32
Type of Residential Remodeler	
General remodeler	49
Design-Build remodeler	46
Specialty contractor	5
2018 Revenue	
Less than $2 million	60
$2 million or more	40
Number of Jobs	
30 jobs or fewer	48
More than 30 jobs	52
Number of Years in Business	
20 years or fewer	45
More than 20 years	55

1. Due to rounding, the numbers in the tables presented throughout the study may not add up to 100 percent.

Ninety-five percent of residential remodelers responding to the survey are either general remodelers (49%) or design-build remodelers (46%). Only 10% are specialty contractors and none are repair/maintenance contractors. In terms of total revenue earned in fiscal year 2018, 60% reported earning less than $2 million and the remaining 40% earned $2 million or more.

When analyzed by the number of jobs completed in 2018, 48% of responding remodelers reported 30 or fewer jobs, while 52% finished more than 30 jobs. A breakdown by tenure in the industry shows that 45 percent have been in business for up to 20 years and the other 55 percent for more than 20 years (Appendix A).

Balance Sheet and Income Statement

The *Remodelers' Cost of Doing Business Study* survey asked remodelers to provide details about their 2018 fiscal year operations. Specifically, participants were asked for the amount of all assets on their 2018 balance sheet (including cash, accounts/note receivables, and other assets), their liabilities (current and long-term), as well as the amount held as owner's equity.

Additionally, and in order to calculate industry-wide averages for gross and net profit margins, respondents were asked for data from their 2018 income statements, including various lines of revenue, costs of sales and operating expenses. In terms of revenue, the survey asked for the amount earned from residential remodeling/repairs, commercial remodeling/repairs, and new single-family home building. It also asked about various costs of sales such as labor, materials, and trade contractors for residential remodeling/repairs, as well as direct construction costs for commercial remodeling and new single-family home building. Data on various operating expenses were also requested, including indirect construction costs, financing

expenses, sales and marketing expenses, general and administrative expenses, and owner's compensation.

To provide historical context for the current findings, this study compares the 2018 data with results from the previous two editions of the *Remodelers' Cost of Doing Business Study* (covering fiscal years 2011 and 2015). As table 1.2 shows, total revenue for residential remodelers in 2018 averaged $2.3 million, 27% higher than the amount reported in 2015 ($1.8 million) and 100% higher than in 2011 ($1.1 million).

In 2018, all costs of sales combined averaged $1.6 million, accounting for 69.9% of revenue. This marks the second consecutive decline in the share of revenue remodelers spend paying for costs of sales (or costs of goods sold) in this series, after spending 73.2% in 2011 and 71.1% in 2015. Looking at each cost category shows that most items took up about the same share of revenue in 2018 as they did in 2015 (materials represented 18.4% of revenue both years, for example), with a couple of exceptions. First, remodelers spent a higher share (28.7%) of their revenue paying for trade contractors in 2018 than in 2015 (25.9%). And second, they spent less (3.0%) on single-family direct construction costs and land in 2018 than in 2015 (5.4%)[2].

Subtracting all costs of sales from revenue shows remodelers with a 2018 gross profit of $682,000, or a 30.1% gross profit margin (682,000 ÷ 2,267,000). This is the highest gross margin remodelers have reported in this series in almost 30 years, since the 38.1% reported in 1990.

After determining gross profits, the next step to figure out net profits is to account for operating expenses. In 2018, these expenses averaged $563,000, or about 24.8% of remodelers' revenue. This means that remodelers spent a higher

---

2. Remodelers in 2018 were significantly less likely to be involved in single-family home building than in 2015. In fact, while 10.4% of their total revenue in 2015 was derived from this secondary activity, the share dropped to 5.6% in 2018.

Table 1.2. Gross Profit						
	2011		2015		2018	
	Average ($1,000s)	Share of revenue (%)	Average ($1,000s)	Share of revenue (%)	Average ($1,000s)	Share of revenue (%)
Revenue	1,134	100.0	1,782	100.0	2,267	100.0
Cost of sales						
Labor for remodeling/repairs*	154	13.5	273	15.3	337	14.8
Materials for remodeling/repairs*	225	19.8	328	18.4	417	18.4
Trade contractors for remodeling/repairs*	326	28.8	462	25.9	650	28.7
Direct costs: commercial remodeling/repairs	28	2.5	38	2.1	13	0.6
Direct costs: single-family and land	62	5.5	96	5.4	68	3.0
Other costs	36	3.2	70	3.9	103	4.5
Total cost of sales	831	73.2	1,266	71.1	1,586	69.9
Gross profit	303	26.8	515	28.9	682	30.1

* Residential

share of their revenue on these items than in 2015 (23.6%) or 2011 (23.7%). In fact, the 24.8% of revenue remodelers spent on operating expenses in 2018 is the second highest in the history of this series, after the 26.7% share reported in 1990 (see Chapter 4).

The growth in expenses between 2015 and 2018 was driven primarily by two items: general and administrative expenses, whose share of revenue rose from 10.6% to 12.6%, and sales and marketing expenses, which went from 2.2% to 3.2% (table 1.3). Other expenses, however, fell or remained unchanged during this period:

Table 1.3. Net Profit						
	2011		2015		2018	
	Average ($1,000s)	Share of revenue (%)	Average ($1,000s)	Share of revenue (%)	Average ($1,000s)	Share of revenue (%)
Gross profit	303	26.8	515	28.9	682	30.1
Operating expenses						
Indirect construction costs	39	3.4	92	5.2	81	3.6
Financing expenses	6	0.6	4	0.2	4	0.2
Sales & mktg. expenses	36	3.2	39	2.2	73	3.2
General & administrative expenses	119	10.5	188	10.6	285	12.6
Owner's compensation	69	6.1	97	5.5	120	5.3
Total operating expenses	269	23.7	420	23.6	563	24.8
Net profit (loss)	34	3.0	95	5.3	118	5.2

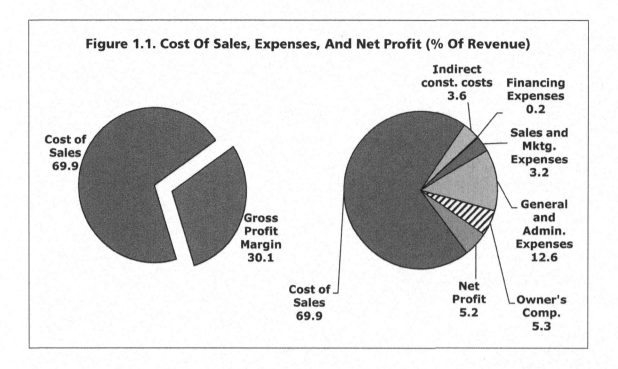

the share spent on indirect construction costs went from 5.2% to 3.6%, owner's compensation slipped slightly from 5.5% to 5.3%, and financing expenses remained stable at 0.2% of revenue. In the end, increased expenses swallowed up higher gross profits to end 2018 with a net profit margin of 5.2%, essentially the same as in 2015 (5.3%), but better than in 2013 (3.0%). Figure 1.1 summarizes remodelers' income statements for 2018.

In addition to the income statement, the *Remodelers' Cost of Doing Business Study* has tracked the balance sheet of remodelers over time. As table 1.4 shows, remodelers responding to the survey had total assets averaging $421,000 in 2018, not significantly higher (about 2%) than in 2015 ($414,000), but an improvement (57%) over assets in 2011 ($269,000)[3].

The plurality of remodelers' assets in 2018 was held as cash ($166,000 or 39.5% of total assets), another 20.9% ($88,000) was tied to accounts and notes receivables, and 13.0% ($55,000) was in the form of other current assets (such as refundable deposits or prepaid expenses). In

all, 73.5% of remodelers' assets were current assets and the other 26.5% were fixed assets.

In an interesting development given the overall (albeit slight) growth in their balance sheets, remodelers' average debt declined significantly between 2015 and 2018, falling 21% from $279,000 to $220,000. Total liabilities represented 52.3% of all assets in 2018, most of which (39.9%) were current liabilities and only a small share (12.4%) long-term liabilities. Looking back at earlier studies in this series shows that 2018 was the year when remodelers relied the least on debt to finance their operations (52.3%), compared to much higher debt-to-asset ratios in 2003 (62.5%), 2011 (65.4%), and 2015 (67.5%).

Meanwhile, on the equity front, remodelers reported the largest average amount of invested capital in 2018, at $200,000. This represented a 48% increase over equity held in 2015 ($135,000) and a 115% increase over 2011 ($93,000). Expressed as a share of total assets, equity financed nearly half (47.7%) of all remodelers' assets in 2018, a reversal in

3. The Remodelers' Cost of Doing Business Study is not designed as a longitudinal survey tracking the same companies over time. Instead, each year's study is based on responses from independent samples of current members of the NAHB.

the steady erosion of this metric in past years: 37.5% in 2003, 34.6% in 2011, and 32.5% in 2015.

Further analysis of remodelers' financial statements, specifically the calculation of the ratios in table 1.5, offers additional insight into the financial health of remodeling companies. Overall, a higher current ratio, lower debt-to-equity ratio, and a stronger ROA (return on assets) show that remodelers were financially stronger companies in 2018 than they were in 2015.

The current ratio is a liquidity measure that evaluates a company's ability to repay its short-term liabilities using its short-term assets. It is calculated by dividing current assets by current liabilities, and in general, the higher the current ratio the healthier the financial state of a company. In 2018, the current ratio for all remodelers responding to the survey was 1.84, which means they had 84% more current assets than current liabilities. This ratio was higher than in 2015 (1.61) and 2011 (1.49).

Another important gauge of a company's financial health is its debt-to-equity ratio. Calculated by dividing total liabilities by total equity, this ratio measures the level of leverage, and therefore risk, that exists in a company. In 2018, remodelers reported an average debt-to-equity ratio of 1.10, which implies they had (only!) 10% more liabilities than invested capital. But more importantly, this finding shows that remodelers cut their reliance on debt by almost half since 2015, when the ratio was 2.07. Prior to 2015, increasing debt levels had taken the ratio from 1.67 in 2003 to 1.90 in 2011. The significant reduction in the debt-to-equity ratio in 2018 bodes well for lower borrowing costs in the future, as institutions pay particular attention to this metric when making lending decisions.

Table 1.4. Balance Sheet						
	2011		2015		2018	
	Average ($1,000s)	Share of total (%)	Average ($1,000s)	Share of total (%)	Average ($1,000s)	Share of total (%)
Assets						
Current assets						
Cash	59	21.9	100	24.1	166	39.5
Accounts/notes receivable	76	28.2	130	31.5	88	20.9
Other current assets	40	14.8	86	20.7	55	13.0
Total current assets	175	65.1	316	76.3	309	73.5
Other assets	94	34.9	98	23.7	112	26.5
Total assets	**269**	**100.0**	**414**	**100.0**	**421**	**100.0**
Liabilities						
Current liabilities	118	43.9	197	47.5	168	39.9
Long term liabilities	58	21.6	83	20.0	52	12.4
Total liabilities	**176**	**65.4**	**279**	**67.5**	**220**	**52.3**
Owner's equity	**93**	**34.6**	**135**	**32.5**	**200**	**47.7**
Total liabilities & owner's equity	**269**	**100.0**	**414**	**100.0**	**421**	**100.0**

Return on assets (ROA) and return on equity (ROE) are two key measures that show how effectively a company is utilizing its assets and invested capital to create profits. In 2018, remodelers were very successful at generating profits out their assets, with an average ROA (net income ÷ total assets) of 28.1%, a higher rate of return than in 2015 (22.9%) or 2011 (12.8%). Meanwhile, their average rate of return on equity, or ROE (net income ÷ total equity), stood at a strong 59.0% in 2018, lower than in 2015 (70.3%) only because equity grew faster than profits during this period.

Table 1.5. Financial Ratios

	2011	2015	2018
Current ratio	1.49	1.61	1.84
Debt-to-equity ratio	1.90	2.07	1.10
Return on assets (%)	12.8	22.9	28.1
Return on equity (%)	37.0	70.3	59.0

Top and Bottom 25%

When looking at profitability benchmarks, it is important to look at averages across the industry, but it is just as critical to understand how the most and least successful quartiles of remodelers performed. This section will show results tabulated separately for two groups of respondents: those in the top 25% in terms of net profit margins and those in the bottom 25% (Appendix B, page 40).

Total revenue among remodelers in the top 25% group averaged $1.6 million in 2018. They spent 68.6% of that on costs of sales, leaving $500,000 in gross profits, a 31.4% gross profit margin. After subtracting operating expenses equivalent to 18.1% of revenue, the average net profit for this most successful set of remodelers was $212,000, a 13.3% net profit margin (fig. 1.2).

Remodelers in the bottom 25% group averaged $2.0 million in revenue in 2018, 70.2% of which was spent on cost of sales. That left $591,000 in gross profits, for a 29.8% gross margin (interestingly, not that much lower than the 31.4% margin posted by the top 25% group). Operating expenses among this least successful group were significantly larger, however, taking up 30.8% of revenue, and driving their net performance into negative territory: a net loss of $20,000, or a net loss margin of −1.0%.

Because the line between the owner's compensation and the business' profit can be blurry in many companies (especially small ones), it is also useful to analyze a broader measure of performance that combines the share of revenue spent on owner's compensation and the net profit margin. As figure 1.2 shows, this overall measure of profitability was 10.5% for all remodelers combined, 16.5% for the top 25%, and 5.6% for the bottom 25%. The latter is further evidence of remodelers' improving financial health in 2018 compared to 2015. That year, even this broader measure of profitability was negative among the bottom 25% group, at −3.9%.

Appendix B shows complete details on income statement differences between remodelers in the most and least successful groups, but two are large enough to deserve a special mention. The bottom 25% of remodelers spent 15.8% of their revenue on general and administrative expenses, a significantly larger share than the 9.7% spent by the top 25%. Similarly, the least successful group spent 6.6% of revenue on the owner's compensation, more than double the 3.2% spent by the most successful group (Appendix B, page 41).

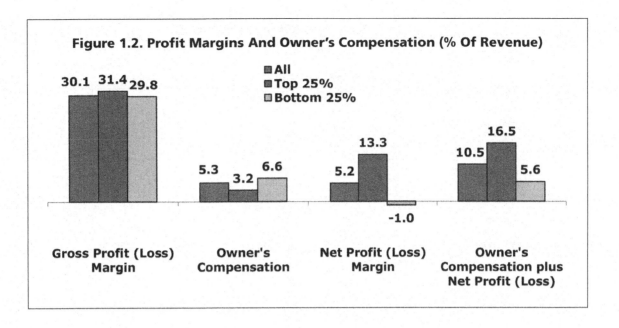

Figure 1.2. Profit Margins And Owner's Compensation (% Of Revenue)

- All
- Top 25%
- Bottom 25%

Gross Profit (Loss) Margin: 30.1, 31.4, 29.8

Owner's Compensation: 5.3, 3.2, 6.6

Net Profit (Loss) Margin: 5.2, 13.3, -1.0

Owner's Compensation plus Net Profit (Loss): 10.5, 16.5, 5.6

The 2018 balance sheet for remodelers in the top 25% group shows they had an average of $306,000 in total assets, $134,000 in total liabilities, and $172,000 in owner's equity. Interestingly, remodelers in the bottom 25% group had slightly larger balance sheets: $335,000 in assets, $174,000 in liabilities, and $161,000 in equity. Table 1.6 summarizes important statistics from the income statement and balance sheet for the top and bottom 25% of respondents.

Profitability for the top 25% group in 2018 was lower than in 2015: the gross margin fell from 35.8% to 31.4%, while the net margin dropped from 16.8% to 13.3%. In addition, and largely due to a sharp reduction in liabilities, this group's current ratio and debt-to-equity ratio saw improvements during this period: the former rose from 3.35 to 3.73 and the latter declined from 0.87 to 0.78. The ROE for the top 25% group in 2018 was an impressive 123.4%, meaning they produced net profits equivalent to 1.23 times the amount of their invested capital!

Although they still lost money, results for the bottom 25% group show some improvement between 2015 and 2018: their gross profit margin rose from 23.1% to 29.8%, while the net profit margin went from −9.9% to −1.0% (just shy of breaking even!). Much like their counterparts in the most successful group, sharply lower levels of debt led their current ratio to rise from 1.10 to 1.95 and the debt-to-equity ratio to drop from 11.34 to 1.07. Net losses kept ROA and ROE in negative territory, but in significantly better positions than in 2015: ROA went from −46.8% to −5.9% while ROE improved from −578.1% to −12.3%.

Table 1.6. Top and Bottom 25%						
	2011		**2015**		**2018**	
	Top 25%	**Bottom 25%**	**Top 25%**	**Bottom 25%**	**Top 25%**	**Bottom 25%**
Gross profit (loss) margin (%)	32.4	24.7	35.8	23.1	31.4	29.8
Net profit (loss) margin (%)	15.9	(3.7)	16.8	(9.9)	13.3	(1.0)
Total assets (thousands $)	189	262	547	293	306	335
Owner's equity (thousands $)	121	4	292	24	172	161
Current ratio	1.90	0.95	3.35	1.10	3.73	1.95
Debt-to-equity ratio	0.56	58.36	0.87	11.34	0.78	1.07
Return on assets (%)	54.8	(19.0)	56.2	(46.8)	69.4	(5.9)
Return on equity (%)	85.6	(1,129.7)	105.3	(578.1)	123.4	(12.3)

2

General Remodelers

Residential remodeling/rehabilitation is a broad industry with four major sub-categories in which businesses can specialize in: general remodeler, design-build remodeler, specialty contractor, and repair & maintenance contractor. This chapter analyzes the financial performance of the nearly half (49%) of respondents who described their firms as general remodelers.

Balance Sheet and Income Statement

General remodelers reported average revenue of $1.6 million in 2018, about 9% lower than in 2015 ($1.8 million), but 44% ahead of 2011 ($1.1 million). Costs of sales were slightly larger in 2018 (72.9%) than in 2015 (71.2%),

driven primarily by a large increase in the share of revenue spent on trade contractors (32.7% vs. 23.5% in 2015). This left a gross profit margin of 27.1%, not far behind where that metric stood in 2015 (28.8%) and still much higher than in 2011 (22.2%) (table 2.1).

Further analysis of their income statements shows that general remodelers managed to keep a tight lid on operating expenses between 2015 and 2018, spending essentially the same share of revenue on these line items: 22.5% vs. 22.2%, respectively. About half of all expenses in 2018 were of a general and administrative nature (11.9%). In the end, despite maintaining stable operating expenses, the weight of a lower

	2011		2015		2018	
Table 2.1. Gross Profit						
	Average ($1,000s)	Share of revenue (%)	Average ($1,000s)	Share of revenue (%)	Average ($1,000s)	Share of revenue (%)
Revenue	1,144	100.0	1,812	100.0	1,642	100.0
Cost of sales						
Labor for remodeling/repairs	156	13.7	301	16.6	219	13.4
Materials for remodeling/repairs	208	18.2	292	16.1	289	17.6
Trade contractors for remodeling/repairs	395	34.5	425	23.5	538	32.7
Direct costs: commercial remodeling/repairs	27	2.3	19	1.1	22	1.3
Direct costs: single-family and land	70	6.1	118	6.5	24	1.4
Other costs	34	3.0	135	7.5	105	6.4
Total cost of sales	890	77.8	1,291	71.2	1,197	72.9
Gross profit	**254**	**22.2**	**521**	**28.8**	**445**	**27.1**

gross profit margin caused general remodelers to have a lower net profit margin in 2018 (4.9%) than in 2015 (6.3%). It should be noted, however, that in 2011 the net profit margin for this subset of remodelers was only 1.8% (table 2.2). Figure 2.1 summarizes the income statement for general remodelers for 2018.

On average, general remodelers had $326,000 worth of assets on their 2018 balance sheets.

Compared to previous studies, that figure was 27% lower than in 2015 ($446,000), but 13% higher than in 2011 ($288,000). In all 78.2% of their assets were held in the form of current assets, with just under half of that held as cash (32.9%). In contrast, in 2011 and 2015, remodelers held much smaller shares of their assets in cash: 20.2% and 21.9%, respectively (table 2.3).

	2011		2015		2018	
	Average ($1,000s)	Share of revenue (%)	Average ($1,000s)	Share of revenue (%)	Average ($1,000s)	Share of revenue (%)
Gross profit	254	22.2	521	28.8	445	27.1
Operating expenses						
Indirect construction costs	35	3.1	116	6.4	69	4.2
Financing expenses	6	0.6	2	0.1	3	0.2
Sales & mktg. expenses	26	2.2	23	1.3	22	1.4
General & administrative expenses	98	8.6	167	9.2	195	11.9
Owner's compensation	68	6.0	99	5.5	75	4.6
Total operating expenses	234	20.4	408	22.5	365	22.2
Net profit (loss)	20	1.8	114	6.3	81	4.9

Table 2.2. Net Profit

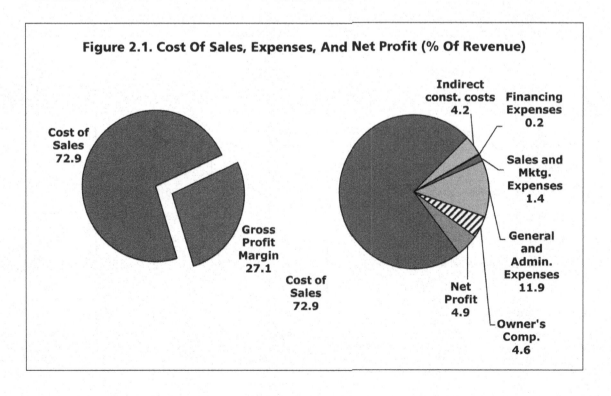

Figure 2.1. Cost Of Sales, Expenses, And Net Profit (% Of Revenue)

On the liability front, general remodelers drastically cut down on the amount of money they owed. On average, this group had liabilities of $167,000 in 2018, 39% less than in 2015 and 4% less than in 2011. Of particular note is their decreased reliance on long-term liabilities to finance their assets: such debt only represented 12.5% of assets, compared to 25.5% in 2015. Meanwhile, owner's equity fell by a much smaller margin than liabilities between 2015 and 2018, dropping only 9% from $174,000 to $158,000. That level of equity, however, backed up nearly half (48.6%) of all the assets general remodelers owned in 2018 — a much higher share than in the previous two studies, when it stood at around 39%.

Lower profit margins and a smaller balance sheet translated into somewhat less positive financial ratios. The average current ratio for

Table 2.3. Balance Sheet

	2011		2015		2018	
	Average ($1,000s)	Share of total (%)	Average ($1,000s)	Share of total (%)	Average ($1,000s)	Share of total (%)
Assets						
Current assets						
Cash	58	20.2	98	21.9	107	32.9
Accounts/notes receivable	96	33.3	160	35.9	83	25.4
Other current assets	39	13.4	126	28.3	65	19.8
Total current assets	193	66.9	384	86.1	255	78.2
Other assets	95	33.1	62	13.9	71	21.8
Total assets	**288**	**100.0**	**446**	**100.0**	**326**	**100.0**
Liabilities						
Current liabilities	126	43.9	158	35.5	127	38.8
Long term liabilities	48	16.6	114	25.5	41	12.5
Total liabilities	**174**	**60.5**	**272**	**61.0**	**167**	**51.4**
Owner's equity	**114**	**39.5**	**174**	**39.0**	**158**	**48.6**
Total liabilities & owner's equity	**288**	**100.0**	**446**	**100.0**	**326**	**100.0**

this group dropped from 2.43 in 2015 to 2.01 in 2018 (although that was still better than the 1.52 reported in 2011), while their ROE dropped from 65.3% to 51.0% (again, still better than the 17.9% reported in 2011) (table 2.4). The rate of return on assets (ROA) also declined, but only slightly, from 25.5% in 2015 to 24.8% in 2018.

General remodelers were successful lowering the level of risk in their companies, however. Their debt-to-equity ratio dropped from the mid 1.50's in 2011 and 2015 to 1.06 in 2018.

Table 2.4. Financial Ratios

	2011	2015	2018
Current ratio	1.52	2.43	2.01
Debt-to-equity ratio	1.53	1.56	1.06
Return on assets (%)	7.1	25.5	24.8
Return on equity (%)	17.9	65.3	51.0

Note: No analysis for the top and bottom 25 percent of general remodelers was produced due to insufficient sample size.

3

Design-Build Remodelers

While 49% of participants in the study described their firms as general remodelers, another important segment of 46% reported they were primarily design-build remodelers. Such companies work with the home owner to provide design and construction services under a single contract. This chapter analyzes the financial performance of this particular subset of respondents.

Balance Sheet and Income Statement

Average total revenue among design-build remodelers increased dramatically for the second time in a row in this series, rising 57% between 2015 and 2018 to $2.9 million, after jumping a similar 56% between 2011 and 2015 (up to $1.8 million). In addition to that substantial level of revenue growth, design-build remodelers in 2018 were also able to reduce costs of sales to their lowest point since results have been tabulated separately for this group (2011), reducing them to 68.4% of revenue — three percentage points below their 2015 share of 71.4% (table 3.1). Given the sharp reduction in costs, design-build remodelers saw their gross profit margin rise to 31.6% in 2018 ($910,000), higher than in both 2015 (28.6%) and 2011 (31.0%).

Table 3.1 Gross Profit						
	2011		2015		2018	
	Average ($1,000s)	Share of revenue (%)	Average ($1,000s)	Share of revenue (%)	Average ($1,000s)	Share of revenue (%)
Revenue	1,171	100.0	1,831	100.0	2,880	100.0
Cost of sales						
Labor for remodeling/repairs	153	13.0	259	14.2	449	15.6
Materials for remodeling/repairs	254	21.7	364	19.9	532	18.5
Trade contractors for remodeling/repairs	284	24.3	544	29.7	773	26.8
Direct costs: commercial remodeling/repairs	29	2.5	23	1.3	4	0.2
Direct costs: single-family and Land	52	4.4	92	5.0	111	3.8
Other costs	36	3.1	25	1.3	102	3.5
Total cost of sales	807	69.0	1,308	71.4	1,971	68.4
Gross profit	**363**	**31.0**	**524**	**28.6**	**910**	**31.6**

In stark contrast to the considerable drop in costs of sales between 2015 and 2018, design-build remodelers saw their operating expenses rise significantly during this period. Altogether, these expenses took up 26.2% of revenue, nearly three percentage points higher than in 2015 (23.4%) (table 3.2). Higher general & administrative expenses were the main culprit, taking up 13.0% of revenue in 2018, com-

pared to 10.7% in 2015. In the end, design-build remodelers reported average net profits of $155,000, for a 5.4% net profit margin — barely ahead of the 5.2% reported in 2015, but still the highest net margin posted by this sub-set of remodelers since first calculated in 2011. Figure 3.1 summarizes the income statement for design-build remodelers for 2018.

Table 3.2 Net Profit						
	2011		2015		2018	
	Average ($1,000s)	Share of revenue (%)	Average ($1,000s)	Share of revenue (%)	Average ($1,000s)	Share of revenue (%)
Gross profit	363	31.0	524	28.6	910	31.6
Operating expenses						
Indirect construction costs	45	3.8	69	3.8	96	3.3
Financing expenses	7	0.6	5	0.3	4	0.1
Sales & mktg. expenses	49	4.2	55	3.0	120	4.2
General & administrative expenses	148	12.6	195	10.7	375	13.0
Owner's compensation	69	5.9	104	5.7	159	5.5
Total operating expenses	318	27.1	428	23.4	754	26.2
Net profit (loss)	46	3.9	95	5.2	155	5.4

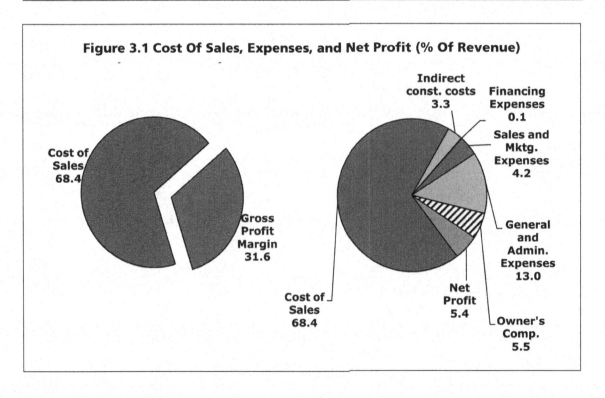

Figure 3.1 Cost Of Sales, Expenses, and Net Profit (% Of Revenue)

Cost of Sales 68.4

Gross Profit Margin 31.6

Indirect const. costs 3.3

Financing Expenses 0.1

Sales and Mktg. Expenses 4.2

General and Admin. Expenses 13.0

Cost of Sales 68.4

Net Profit 5.4

Owner's Comp. 5.5

Meanwhile, the balance sheet of the average design-build remodeler in 2018 showed $459,000 in total assets, 12% higher than in 2015 ($411,000) and nearly 120% ahead of 2011 ($210,000). As was the case among general remodelers, design-build remodelers have also experienced a significant increase in their cash position recently. In fact, between 2015 and 2018, their share of assets held in cash doubled from 23.2% 46.8% (table 3.3).

Another variation that is common to both groups of remodelers is the recent decline in overall liabilities. Total debt for design-build remodelers in 2018 reached $250,000, 17% less than in 2015 ($302,000). Their debt structure has also steadily shifted away from long-

term liabilities, which have gone from representing 22.7% of assets in 2011, to 14.7% in 2015, and to 9.5% in 2018.

One balance sheet feature that is unique to design-build remodelers, however, is their continued investment of capital in their firms. In 2018, they had an average of $209,000 in equity, almost twice the average in 2015 ($109,000), and almost 300% more than in 2011 ($53,000). This strong increase led investment capital to be the source of financing for 45.5% of all this group's assets in 2018, up from only 26.6% in 2015.

Financially speaking, design-build remodelers were much stronger in 2018 than in 2015.

Table 3.3. Balance Sheet						
	2011		2015		2018	
	Average ($1,000s)	Share of total (%)	Average ($1,000s)	Share of total (%)	Average ($1,000s)	Share of total (%)
Assets						
Current assets						
Cash	62	29.6	95	23.2	215	46.8
Accounts/notes receivable	62	29.6	113	27.5	74	16.1
Other current assets	41	19.4	68	16.6	49	10.7
Total current assets	165	78.6	276	67.2	338	73.6
Other assets	45	21.4	135	32.8	121	26.4
Total assets	210	100.0	411	100.0	459	100.0
Liabilities						
Current liabilities	109	52	241	58.7	206	44.9
Long term liabilities	48	22.7	60	14.7	44	9.5
Total liabilities	157	74.7	302	73.4	250	54.5
Owner's equity	53	25.3	109	26.6	209	45.5
Total liabilities & owner's equity	210	100.0	411	100.0	459	100.0

The combination of higher current assets and lower current liabilities improved their current ratio from 1.14 to 1.64. Fewer debts and more invested capital led their debt-to-equity ratio to fall by more than half, from 2.76 to 1.20 during this period. ROA rose from 23.2% to 33.9%, while returns on equity were solid at 74.3% (table 3.4).

Table 3.4. Financial Ratios			
	2011	2015	2018
Current ratio	1.51	1.14	1.64
Debt-to-equity ratio	2.96	2.76	1.20
Return on assets (%)	21.8	23.2	33.9
Return on equity (%)	86.4	87.3	74.3

Note: *No analysis for the top and bottom 25 percent of design-build remodelers was produced due to insufficient sample size.*

Comparison across Regions, Business Models, & Historical Trends

This chapter offers readers a chance to look at the results in a different light by comparing profitability and asset benchmarks across regions of the country (only the South and West regions provided enough data to produce results separately) and across the two business models addressed in previous chapters (general remodelers and design-build remodelers). Historical data for all the previous *Remodelers' Cost of Doing Business Studies* produced by the NAHB are also included to identify relevant trends over time.

Revenue & Profits by Region

Among all remodelers participating in the study, an average of 89% of the income received in 2018 came from doing residential remodeling/repair work, about 6% from new single-family home building, 2% from commercial remodeling/repairs, and the remaining 3% from 'other' lines of business. Remodelers in the South region reported an average of $2.0 million in total revenue, of which 83% came from residential remodeling work and 10% from new single-family home building. Revenue was significantly larger among remodelers in the West, at $3.1 million, with 89% of it coming from residential remodeling and only 7% from new single-family home building (Appendix A, page 37).

The cost of labor, material, and trade contractors for residential remodeling/repairs took up a slightly higher share of revenue in the South (61.1%) than in the West (59.5%) (fig. 4.1). Of all costs of sales, trade contractors were the most expensive item for remodelers, accounting for 30.4% of revenue in the South and for 26.7% in the West. After subtracting all costs of sales, remodelers in the South and West regions reported rather similar gross profit margins, at 29.6% and 29.0%, respectively.

In terms of operating expenses, remodelers in the South spent a smaller share of their revenue on general & administrative expenses (12.9%) than those in the West (15.0%), but paid slightly more for indirect construction costs (3.8% vs. 2.1%, respectively) and for owner's compensation (5.3% vs. 4.3%, respectively). Altogether, remodelers in the South spent a slightly larger share of revenue on operating expenses (25.1%) than those in the West (24.1%). In the end, the bottom line (before taxes) was strikingly similar for remodelers in both regions: those in the South averaged a 4.6% net profit margin, compared to 5.0% among those in the West.

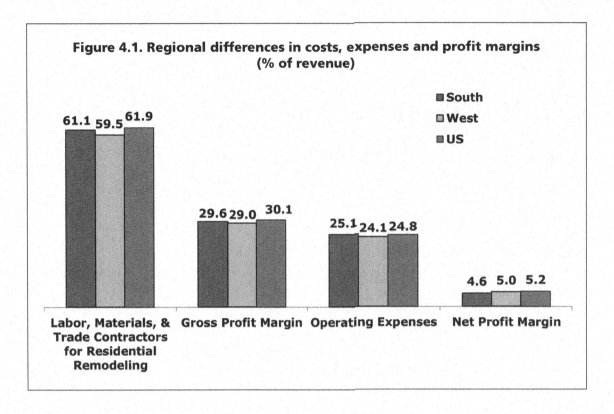

Figure 4.1. Regional differences in costs, expenses and profit margins (% of revenue)

Revenue & Profits by Business Model

The *Remodelers' Cost of Doing Business Study* produced results separately for general remodelers and design-build remodelers for the first time in 2011. That year, design-build remodelers posted a higher net profit margin (3.9%) than general remodelers (1.8%). In 2015, the roles were reversed, as general remodelers were somewhat more profitable (6.3%) than design-build remodelers (5.2%). In 2018, the top spot flipped again, with design-build remodelers averaging a 5.4% net margin, slightly ahead of the 4.9% posted by general remodelers (fig.4.2).

Design-build remodelers averaged $2.9 million in revenue in 2018, about 75% more than the average $1.6 million generated by general remodelers. Design-build remodelers generated 91% of their revenue from residential remodeling/repair work and 5% from new

single-family home building. Those shares were 85% and 8%, respectively, among general remodelers.

The cost of labor, materials, and trade contractors for residential remodeling work took up a larger share of revenue from general remodelers (63.7%) than it did from design-build remodelers (60.9%), driven primarily by the high cost of trade contractors. The latter cost general remodelers 32.7% of revenue, compared to 26.8% among design-trade contractors. After subtracting all costs of sales, design build-remodelers had a higher gross profit margin (31.6%) than general remodelers (27.1%) (Appendix A, page 37).

Exactly the opposite of the trend for costs of sales, design-build remodelers spent more on operating expenses (26.2% of revenue) than did general remodelers (22.2%). The most significant discrepancy between the two groups in this section of the income statement is in the share of revenue each spent on sales & marketing expenses: 4.2% among design-build remodelers, compared to only 1.4% among general remodelers. Design-build remodelers also paid their owners 5.5% of revenue, about 1 percentage point more than general remodelers (4.6%).

Despite their higher operating expenses, design-build remodelers' stronger gross profit margin gave them an edge to finish 2018 with a net profit margin of 5.4%, slightly higher than the 4.9% reported by general remodelers. Looking at the broader measure of profitability that combines net margins and owner's compensation together shows a somewhat larger performance gap between design-build (10.9%) and (9.5%) general remodelers.

Design-build remodelers held $459,000 worth of assets in 2018, about 40% more than did general remodelers ($326,000) (fig. 4.3).

Design-build remodelers had $215,000 of their assets in cash (46.8%), $74,000 in account and notes receivables (16.1%), $49,000 in other current assets (10.7%), and the remaining $121,000 in fixed assets (26.4%). In comparison, general remodelers only held $107,000 in cash (32.9%), another $83,000 in accounts and notes receivable (25.4%), $65,000 in other current assets (19.8%), and $71,000 in fixed assets (21.8%) (Appendix A, page 35).

Meanwhile, design-build remodelers' total liabilities (both current and long-term) and equity averaged $250,000 and $209,000, respectively, which implies that 54.5% of their assets were financed through debt and only 45.5% through invested capital. Among general remodelers, average liabilities reached $167,000, financing a smaller share of assets (51.4%), while $158,000 in owner's equity financed the remaining 48.6%.

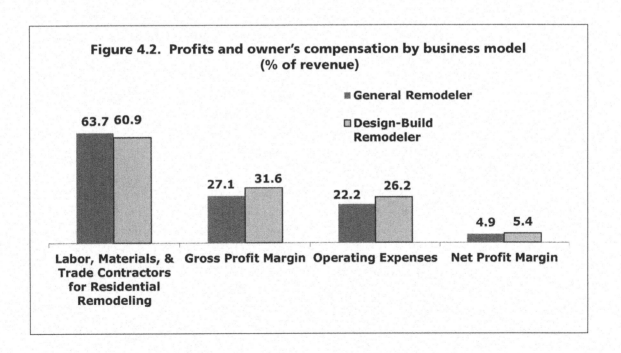

Figure 4.2. Profits and owner's compensation by business model (% of revenue)

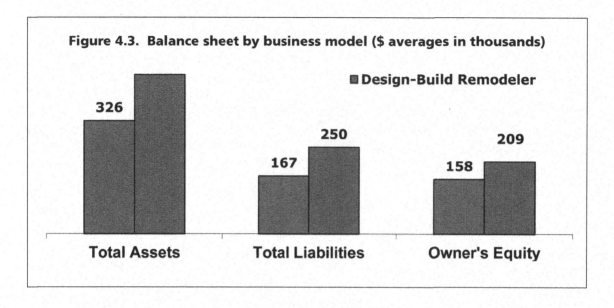

Figure 4.3. Balance sheet by business model ($ averages in thousands)

A comparison of key financial ratios between the two business models shows that general remodelers outperformed their design-build counterparts in debt-related metrics but not in those measuring rates of return. For example, general remodelers' current ratio in 2018 was 2.01, moderately higher than the 1.64 ratio posted by design-build remodelers (table 4.1). In terms of their reliance on debt to finance their businesses, general remodelers reported a slightly lower debt-to-equity ratio (1.06) than design-build remodelers (1.20).

When it comes to squeezing profits out of assets and equity, however, design-build remodelers were relatively more successful. Their return on assets (ROA) was 33.9%, compared to 24.8% among general remodelers, while their respective returns on equity (ROE) were 74.3% and 51.0%.

Historical Trends

The *Remodelers' Cost of Doing Business Study* has been conducted periodically since 1990. That year, the average net profit margin for this segment of the industry was reported at 11.4% (the highest in the series). In both 1993 and 1996, remodelers reported an average net profit margin of 6.8%, but in the next two iterations of the study, in 2003 and 2011, the net margin declined to 4.2% and 3.0%, respectively. The downward trend was reversed in 2015, however, when the average net margin rose to 5.3%. The data collected for fiscal year 2018 shows this metric essentially flat, at 5.2% (table 4.2).

Throughout much of the history of this study (from 1993 to 2015), remodelers have spent between 71% and 73% of their revenue on the various items under costs of sales (e.g. labor, material, and trade contractors). In 2018, costs of sales fell under 70% for only the second time in the series — down to 69.9% (the only other time was in 1990, at 61.9%). Given these trends in costs, remodelers' gross profit margins have mostly hovered just under 30%, except for 1990 (38.1%) and now 2018 (30.1%).

Table 4.1. Financial Ratios		
	General Remodelers	Design-Build Remodelers
Current ratio	2.01	1.64
Debt-to-equity ratio	1.06	1.20
Return on assets (%)	24.8	33.9
Return on equity (%)	51.0	74.3

Operating expenses were highest in 1990, when they accounted for 26.7% of all revenue. By 1993, remodelers had greatly tightened the belt around these expenses, driving them down to only 21.9% of revenue. Most years since, they have taken up about 22% or 23% of revenue. In 2018, however, these expenses rose to represent 24.8% of remodelers' revenue — the highest share since 1990.

Table 4.2. Historical Comparison of Profitability (% of Revenue)					
	Total Revenue	Cost of Sales	Gross Profit Margin	Operating Expenses	Net Profit Margin
2018	100	69.9	30.1	24.8	5.2
2015	100	71.1	28.9	23.6	5.3
2011	100	73.2	26.8	23.7	3.0
2003	100	71.6	28.4	24.3	4.2
1996	100	71.0	29.0	22.2	6.8
1993	100	71.3	28.7	21.9	6.8
1990	100	61.9	38.1	26.7	11.4

5

Operations

Main Operation

Residential remodeling/rehabilitation was the main operation of 95% of survey respondents in 2018 (fig 5.1). About 3% were single-family home builders, and 2% were commercial remodelers. As stated earlier, only respondents whose primary operation was residential remodeling were included in the financial analysis presented throughout this report.

Type of Residential Remodeler

Just under half (49%) of all residential remodelers responding to the survey described their firms as general remodelers, 46% as design-build remodelers, and 5% as specialty contractors. Pairing this data with financial statements, it is also possible to explore what type of remodelers made up the most successful group (top 25% in terms of net profit margins) as well as the least successful one (bottom 25%).

Figure 5.2 shows that general remodelers represented the majority — 55% — of the firms in the top 25% group, but only 27% of those in the bottom 25%. On the contrary, design-build remodelers made up 45% of the top 25% group, but the majority (73%) of those in the bottom 25%. No specialty contractor cracked either the top 25% or the bottom 25% groups (Appendix B, page 42).

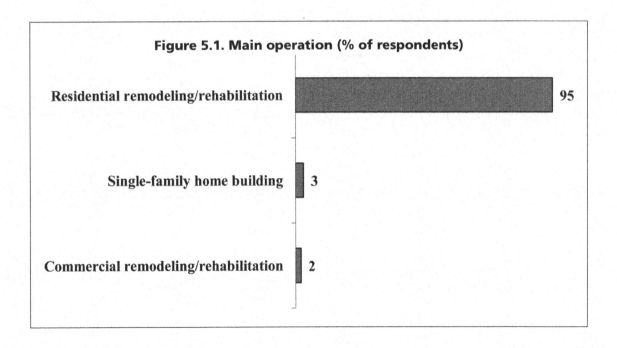

Figure 5.1. Main operation (% of respondents)

Residential remodeling/rehabilitation	95
Single-family home building	3
Commercial remodeling/rehabilitation	2

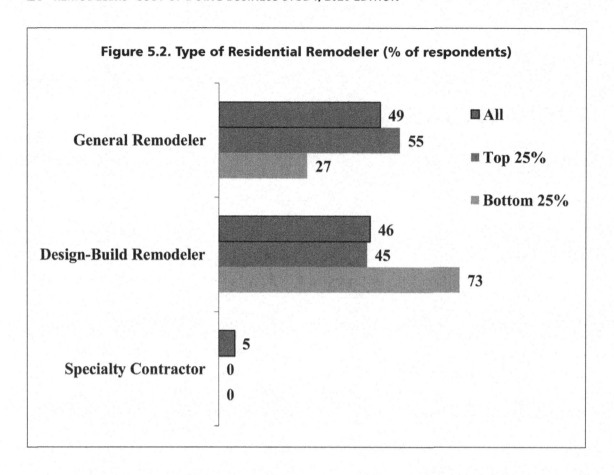

Figure 5.2. Type of Residential Remodeler (% of respondents)

Number of Years in Business

Residential remodelers responding to the survey have been in business for an average of 25 years. Twenty percent have been in the business for up to 10 years, 20% for 11 to 19 years, another 20% for 20 to 29 years, but the plurality — 41% — have been residential remodelers for 30 years or longer (fig. 5.3).

Remodelers in the top 25% group have been in business for an average of 24 years, one less than the average among those in the bottom 25% (25 years). More than 50% of each group have been in business for at least 20 years (Appendix B, page 42).

Remodelers with more than 20 years of experience reported a gross profit margin of 30.1%, essentially the same as the 30.0% reported by those with less experience (up to 20 years in business). Operating expenses, however, were somewhat higher for the less experienced group (26.3% vs. 24.2%), leading them to a net profit margin of 3.7%. Remodelers with more than 20 years in the business reported a larger average net profit margin of 5.9% (Appendix A, page 37).

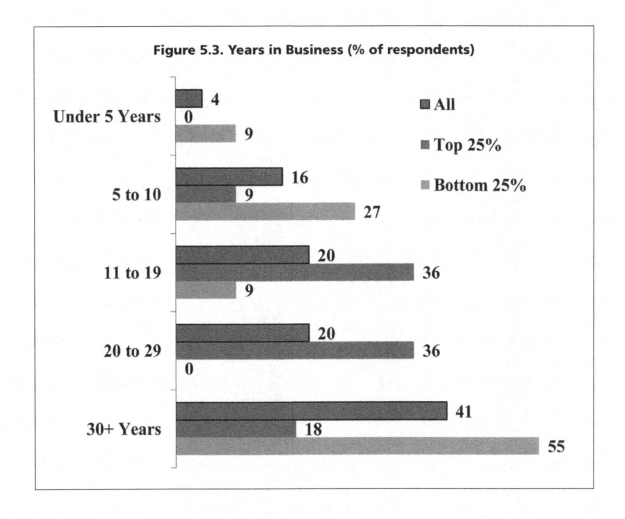

Figure 5.3. Years in Business (% of respondents)

Legend:
■ All
■ Top 25%
■ Bottom 25%

Under 5 Years: All 4, Top 25% 0, Bottom 25% 9
5 to 10: All 16, Top 25% 9, Bottom 25% 27
11 to 19: All 20, Top 25% 36, Bottom 25% 9
20 to 29: All 20, Top 25% 36, Bottom 25% 0
30+ Years: All 41, Top 25% 18, Bottom 25% 55

Number of Jobs Completed

Residential remodelers were also asked about the number of jobs completed during 2018 in each of four different price ranges. On average, remodelers completed 23 jobs priced at under $5,000, 18 jobs priced between $5,000 and $24,999, 21 jobs priced between $25,000 and $99,999, and 7 jobs worth $100,000 or more. Altogether, remodelers completed an average of 69 jobs in 2018[4] (fig. 5.4). Remodelers with net profit margins in the top quartile completed an average of only 23 jobs in 2018: 5 worth $100,000 or more and 6 in each of the lower price ranges. Remodelers in the lowest quartile, in contrast, completed 56 jobs, more than twice the number of the most successful group. The majority of those jobs — 29 — were small jobs under $5,000 and only 6 were for $100,000 or more.

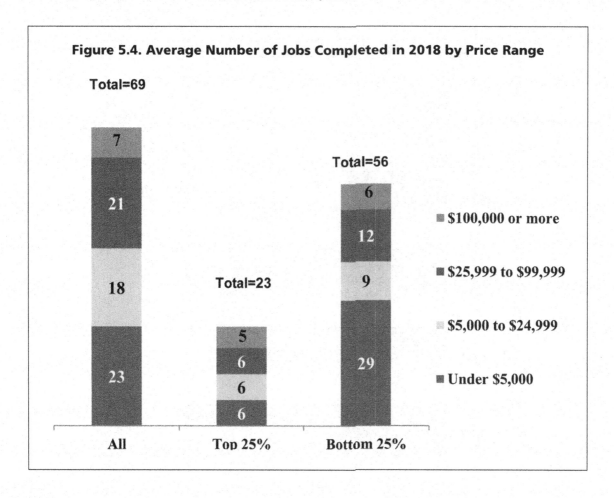

Figure 5.4. Average Number of Jobs Completed in 2018 by Price Range

Number of Full-Time Employees

An analysis of the number of jobs completed by business model shows that, on average, design-build remodelers finished 53 jobs in 2018, ahead of the 47 finished by general remodelers. Regionally, respondents in the South reported completing 77 jobs, compared to 65 jobs by remodelers in the West. Remodelers with more than 20 years in the business finished 87 jobs, almost twice as many as those with less tenure (47 jobs) jobs (Appendix A, page 34).

Meanwhile, profitability and the number of jobs completed showed an inverse relationship in 2018. Remodelers who finished 30 or fewer jobs posted a net profit margin of 6.2%, compared to a lower 4.2% among those who finished more than 30 jobs (Appendix A, page 37).

The survey also included a question inquiring about the number of full-time employees on payroll in 2018. The question instructed the respondent to include himself or herself in the count, and if the firm had any part-time employees, to use full-time equivalents (that is, number of paid hours divided by 2,080 hours). Residential remodelers who participated in the study had an average of 10.2 employees on payroll in 2018. Of them, 5.8 worked in the field, 2.9 worked in the office, and 1.6 in sales. Fourteen percent reported having up to 2.0 full-time positions (or equivalents), another 11% had 2.1 to 4 positions, 18% had 4.1 to 6.0, 21% had 6.1 to 10, 16% 10.1 to 15, and 21% had more than 15 employees on payroll (fig. 5.5).

4. In 2015, remodelers completed an average of 54 jobs. Among the top 25% group the average was 44, while among the bottom 25%, it was 40.

Looking at the average number of employees across the top and bottom 25% quartiles shows that the most successful group of remodelers had about half as many employees (5.5) as did the least successful group (12.0). In fact, while 36% of remodelers in the bottom 25% had more than 15 employees, only 9% of those in the top 25% reported such a large payroll (Appendix B, page 43).

Design-build remodelers had 11.0 full-time employees (or equivalents) in 2018, com-pared to 8.4 among general remodelers. Across regions, remodelers in the West had 11.7 employees, compared to 8.5 in the South. Those with more than 20 years in business reported an average of 12.0 employees, com-pared to only 8.2 among those with up to 20 years as remodelers. Meanwhile, remodelers whose income in 2018 was under $2 million reported a total of 6.6 full-time positions, com-pared to 14.8 among those earning $2 million or more (Appendix A, page 34).

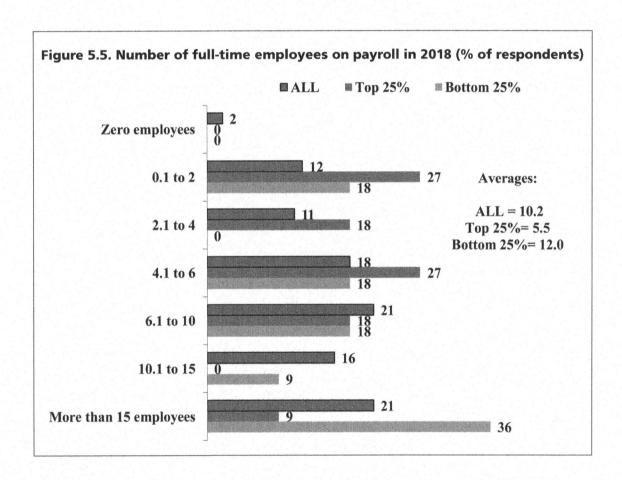

Figure 5.5. Number of full-time employees on payroll in 2018 (% of respondents)

ALL   Top 25%   Bottom 25%

Averages:

ALL = 10.2
Top 25% = 5.5
Bottom 25% = 12.0

APPENDIX

A

Detailed Tables

Q1a. Indicate your Firms Main Operation During Fiscal 2018
(Percent of Respondents)

	Total	Region		Type of Residential Remodeler		Total 2018 Revenue		Number of Jobs		Number of years in Business	
		South	West	General	Design-Build	< $2 million	≥ $2 million	≤ 30	> 30	≤ 20	> 20
Residential remodeling/ rehabilitation	95	100	100	100	96	100	100	91	100	96	94
Commercial remodeling/ rehabilitation	2				4			3		4	3
Single-family home building	3							6			3

Q1b. Percent of your business from each operation
(Average Share)

	Total	Region		Type of Residential Remodeler		Total 2018 Revenue		Number of Jobs		Number of years in Business	
		South	West	General	Design-Build	< $2 million	≥ $2 million	≤ 30	> 30	≤ 20	> 20
Residential remodeling/rehabilitation	86	86	88	87	90	92	90	84	89	85	87
Commercial remodeling/rehabilitation	6	4	5	6	5	3	5	8	3	4	7
Single-family home building	6	7	3	2	5	2	5	6	5	5	6
Multifamily home building	0	0	0	0	0	0	0	0	0	0	0
Other	2	4	3	5	1	3	0	1	4	5	0

Q2. *If a Residential Remodeler, please indicate best description of the firm*
(Percent of Respondents)

	Total	Region		Type of Residential Remodeler		Total 2018 Revenue		Number of Jobs		Number of years in Business	
		South	West	General	Design-Build	< $2 million	≥ $2 million	≤ 30	> 30	≤ 20	> 20
General remodeler	49	52	61	100		57	32	60	37	58	42
Design-Build remodeler	46	38	39		100	39	68	40	52	38	52
Specialty contractor	5	10				4			11	4	6

Q3. *Years Firm Has Been in Residential Remodeling Business.*
(Percent of Respondents)

	Total	Region		Type of Residential Remodeler		Total 2018 Revenue		Number of Jobs		Number of years in Business	
		South	West	General	Design-Build	< $2 million	≥ $2 million	≤ 30	> 30	≤ 20	> 20
Under 5 years	4	10		4	4	4		3	4	8	
5-10 years	16	15	17	19	12	15	16	17	15	36	
11-19 years	20	30	11	19	23	30	11	17	22	44	
20-29 years	20	15	33	26	8	22	5	14	26	12	26
30+ Years	41	30	39	33	54	30	68	48	33		74
Average (Years)	25	21	27	23	27	23	30	25	24	12	35

Q4. How many jobs in each of these price ranges did your firm complete in 2018?
(Average Number of Jobs)

	Total	Region		Type of Residential Remodeler		Total 2018 Revenue		Number of Jobs		Number of years in Business	
		South	West	General	Design-Build	< $2 million	≥ $2 million	≤ 30	> 30	≤ 20	> 20
Under $5,000	23	16	31	26	17	27	8	3	42	15	30
$5,000 to $24,999	18	26	12	6	16	8	17	5	30	10	24
$25,000 to $99,999	21	29	11	11	11	16	11	3	37	18	23
$100,000 or more	7	6	11	4	10	2	15	6	8	4	9
Average # of Jobs	69	77	65	47	53	53	52	17	117	47	87
Median # of Jobs	32	30	33	28	33	28	28	17	55	35	28

Q5. On avearge, how many full-time employees (including yourself) did your firm have on payroll in 2018?
(Percent of Respondents)

	Total	Region		Type of Residential Remodeler		Total 2018 Revenue		Number of Jobs		Number of years in Business	
		South	West	General	Design-Build	< $2 million	≥ $2 million	≤ 30	> 30	≤ 20	> 20
Average # of Employees											
Office	2.9	2.1	4.0	2.2	3.5	1.6	4.3	2.5	3.3	1.8	3.8
Field	5.8	4.7	6.3	5.6	5.8	4.2	8.3	5.1	6.5	5.4	6.0
Sales	1.6	1.7	1.4	0.7	1.8	0.8	2.2	0.9	2.4	0.9	2.1
Total Average	**10.2**	**8.5**	**11.7**	**8.4**	**11.0**	**6.6**	**14.8**	**8.5**	**12.2**	**8.2**	**12.0**
Percent of Respondents											
Zero employees	2	5		4				3		4	
0.1 to 2	12	24		21	4	25		23		12	13
2.1 to 4	11	14	6	11	12	14		10	11	12	10
4.1 to 6	18	10	33	21	15	21	11	17	19	27	10
6.1 to 10	21	19	11	14	27	18	21	13	30	23	19
10.1 to 15	16	14	22	14	19	14	26	13	19	8	23
More than 15 employees	21	14	28	14	23	7	42	20	22	15	26
Median	8	6	10	6	9	5	13	6	10	6	10

Q6. Balance Sheet
(Average in $1,000s)

	Total	Region		Type of Residential Remodeler		Total 2018 Revenue		Number of Jobs		Number of years in Business	
		South	West	General	Design-Build	< $2 million	≥ $2 million	≤ 30	> 30	≤ 20	> 20
Assets											
Cash	166	137	221	107	215	92	255	140	198	119	199
Accounts and notes receivables	88	112	135	83	74	28	125	72	107	45	118
Other current assets	55	36	104	65	49	27	94	62	46	59	51
Other assets	112	94	88	71	121	82	132	73	158	91	126
Total assets	**421**	**378**	**548**	**326**	**459**	**230**	**606**	**347**	**509**	**314**	**494**
Liabilities											
Current liabilities	168	147	233	127	206	75	272	133	209	124	198
Long-term liabilities	52	34	86	41	44	55	43	37	70	55	51
Owner's Equity	200	197	229	158	209	100	291	176	230	135	245
Total Liabilities + Equity	**421**	**378**	**548**	**326**	**459**	**230**	**606**	**347**	**509**	**314**	**494**

Q7. Income Statement
(Average in $1,000s)

	Total	Region		Type of Residential Remodeler		Total 2018 Revenue		Number of Jobs		Number of years in Business	
		South	West	General	Design-Build	< $2 million	≥ $2 million	≤ 30	> 30	≤ 20	> 20
Revenue											
Residential remodeling/repairs	2,028	1,636	2,765	1,403	2,633	1,004	3,538	1,814	2,318	1,339	2,586
Commercial remodeling/repairs	36	7	34	58	17	30	46	46	23	46	28
New single-family home building	128	190	226	127	134	30	272	30	261	136	122
All Other Revenue	75	127	71	54	97	47	115	74	75	63	84
Total Company Revenue	2,267	1,960	3,096	1,642	2,880	1,111	3,970	1,963	2,677	1,583	2,819
Cost of Sales											
Labor for residential remodeling/ repairs (inc. fringe benefits)	337	244	513	219	449	168	585	267	431	257	401
Materials for residential remodeling/repairs	417	357	501	289	532	215	714	345	513	343	476
Trade Contractors for residential remodeling/repairs	650	596	827	538	773	246	1,244	694	590	347	894
Commercial remodeling and repairs direct construction costs	13	8	9	22	4	15	9	18	5	15	10
New single-family direct construction costs and Land	68	45	179	24	111	24	132	19	133	32	96
All other costs of sales	103	129	168	105	102	35	202	106	97	114	93
Total Company Cost of Sales	1,586	1,379	2,197	1,197	1,971	704	2,885	1,450	1,769	1,108	1,971
Gross Profit	682	581	899	445	910	408	1,085	514	908	475	848
Operating Expenses											
Indirect construction costs	81	74	66	69	96	61	111	73	93	83	80
Financing Expenses	4	5	5	3	4	4	4	3	5	4	4
Sales and Marketing Expenses	73	55	75	22	120	27	141	32	128	34	105
General and Administrative Expenses	285	253	466	195	375	161	467	171	439	201	353
Owner's Compensation	120	104	132	75	159	76	186	113	130	95	141
Total Operating Expenses	563	491	745	365	754	329	909	392	794	416	682
Net Income Before Taxes	118	90	154	81	155	79	176	122	114	59	166

Q7. Income Statement
(Share of Revenue)

	Total	Region		Type of Residential Remodeler		Total 2018 Revenue		Number of Jobs		Number of years in Business	
		South	West	General	Design-Build	> $2 million	≥ $2 million	≤ 30	> 30	≤ 20	> 20
Revenue											
Residential remodeling/repairs	89.5	83.4	89.3	85.4	91.4	90.4	89.1	92.4	86.6	84.6	91.7
Commercial remodeling/repairs	1.6	0.4	1.1	3.6	0.6	2.7	1.1	2.3	0.9	2.9	1.0
New single-family home building	5.6	9.7	7.3	7.7	4.6	2.7	6.8	1.5	9.7	8.6	4.3
All Other Revenue	3.3	6.5	2.3	3.3	3.4	4.2	2.9	3.8	2.8	4.0	3.0
Total Company Revenue	100.0	100.0	100.0	100.0	100.0	100.0	100.0	100.0	100.0	100.0	100.0
Cost of Sales											
Labor for residential remodeling/ repairs (inc. fringe benefits)	14.8	12.4	16.6	13.4	15.6	15.2	14.7	13.6	16.1	16.2	14.2
Materials for residential remodeling/repairs	18.4	18.2	16.2	17.6	18.5	19.3	18.0	17.6	19.2	21.6	16.9
Trade Contractors for residential remodeling/repairs	28.7	30.4	26.7	32.7	26.8	22.1	31.3	35.4	22.0	21.9	31.7
Commercial remodeling and repairs direct construction costs	0.6	0.4	0.3	1.3	0.2	1.3	0.2	0.9	0.2	1.0	0.4
New single-family direct construction costs and Land	3.0	2.3	5.8	1.4	3.8	2.2	3.3	1.0	5.0	2.0	3.4
All other costs of sales	4.5	6.6	5.4	6.4	3.5	3.2	5.1	5.4	3.6	7.2	3.3
Total Company Cost of Sales	69.9	70.4	71.0	72.9	68.4	63.3	72.7	73.8	66.1	70.0	69.9
Gross Profit	**30.1**	**29.6**	**29.0**	**27.1**	**31.6**	**36.7**	**27.3**	**26.2**	**33.9**	**30.0**	**30.1**
Operating Expenses											
Indirect construction costs	3.6	3.8	2.1	4.2	3.3	5.5	2.8	3.7	3.5	5.2	2.8
Financing Expenses	0.2	0.2	0.2	0.2	0.1	0.3	0.1	0.2	0.2	0.2	0.1
Sales and Marketing Expenses	3.2	2.8	2.4	1.4	4.2	2.4	3.6	1.7	4.8	2.2	3.7
General and Administrative Expenses	12.6	12.9	15.0	11.9	13.0	14.5	11.8	8.7	16.4	12.7	12.5
Owner's Compensation	5.3	5.3	4.3	4.6	5.5	6.8	4.7	5.8	4.9	6.0	5.0
Total Operating Expenses	24.8	25.1	24.1	22.2	26.2	29.6	22.9	20.0	29.7	26.3	24.2
Net Income Before Taxes	**5.2**	**4.6**	**5.0**	**4.9**	**5.4**	**7.1**	**4.4**	**6.2**	**4.2**	**3.7**	**5.9**

All Residential Remodelers Top and Bottom 25% by Net Profit Margin

Income statement
(average in $1,000s)

	ALL	Top 25%	Bottom 25%
Revenue			
Residential remodeling/repairs	2,028	1,452	1,732
Commercial remodeling/repairs	36	30	10
New single-family home building	128	51	182
All other revenue	75	58	60
Total company revenue	2,267	1,591	1,983
Costs of sales			
Labor for residential remodeling/repairs	337	206	378
Materials for residential remodeling/repairs	417	297	481
Trade Contractors for residential remodeling/repairs	650	387	418
Commercial remodeling and repairs direct construction costs	13	3	8
New single-family direct construction costs and land	68	37	0
All other costs of sales	103	160	108
Total cost of sales	1,586	1,091	1,393
Gross profit	**682**	**500**	**591**
Operating expenses			
Indirect construction costs	81	59	94
Financing expenses	4	3	7
Sales and marketing expenses	73	19	68
General and administrative expenses	285	155	312
Owner's compensation	120	52	130
Total operating expenses	563	288	611
Net income before taxes	**118**	**212**	**(20)**

Income Statement
(% share of revenue)

	ALL	Top 25%	Bottom 25%
Revenue			
Residential remodeling/repairs	89.5	91.3	87.3
Commercial remodeling/repairs	1.6	1.9	0.5
New single-family home building	5.6	3.2	9.2
All other revenue	3.3	3.7	3.0
Total company revenue	100.0	100.0	100.0
Costs of sales			
Labor for residential remodeling/repairs	14.8	13.0	19.1
Materials for residential remodeling/repairs	18.4	18.7	24.3
Trade Contractors for residential remodeling/repairs	28.7	24.3	21.1
Commercial remodeling and repairs direct construction costs	0.6	0.2	0.4
New single-family direct construction costs and land	3.0	2.3	0.0
All other costs of sales	4.5	10.1	5.4
Total cost of sales	69.9	68.6	70.2
Gross profit	**30.1**	**31.4**	**29.8**
Operating expenses			
Indirect construction costs	3.6	3.7	4.7
Financing expenses	0.2	0.2	0.3
Sales and marketing expenses	3.2	1.2	3.4
General and administrative expenses	12.6	9.7	15.8
Owner's compensation	5.3	3.2	6.6
Total operating expenses	24.8	18.1	30.8
Net income before taxes	**5.2**	**13.3**	**(1.0)**

Balance Sheet
(average in $1,000s)

	ALL	Top 25%	Bottom 25%
Assets			
Cash	166	132	114
Accounts and notes receivables	88	65	42
Other current assets	55	81	74
Other assets	112	28	105
Total assets	**421**	**306**	**335**
Liabilities			
Current liabilities	168	74	118
Long-term liabilities	52	59	56
Owner's Equity	200	172	161
Total Liabilities + Equity	**421**	**306**	**335**

Please indicate best description of the firm
(Percent of Respondents)

	ALL	Top 25%	Bottom 25%
General remodeler	49	55	27
Design-Build remodeler	46	45	73
Specialty contractor	5		

Years Firm Has Been in Residential Remodeling Business
(Percent of Respondents)

	ALL	Top 25%	Bottom 25%
Under 5 years	4		9
5-10 years	16	9	27
11-19 years	20	36	9
20-29 years	20	36	
30+ Years	41	18	55
Average (Years)	25	24	25

How many jobs in each of these price ranges did your firm complete in 2018?
(Average Number of Jobs)

	ALL	Top 25%	Bottom 25%
Under $5,000	23	6	29
$5,000 to $24,999	18	6	9
$25,000 to $99,999	21	6	12
$100,000 or more	7	5	6
Average Total # of Jobs	69	22	55

On avearge, how many full-time employees (including yourself) did your firm have on payroll in 2018?

Average # of Employees	ALL	Top 25%	Bottom 25%
Office	2.9	1.8	2.6
Field	5.8	3.3	8.0
Sales	1.6	0.4	1.3
Total Average	**10.2**	**5.5**	**12.0**
Percent of Respondents			
Zero employees	2		
0.1 to 2	12	27	18
2.1 to 4	11	18	
4.1 to 6	18	27	18
6.1 to 10	21	18	18
10.1 to 15	16		9
More than 15 employees	21	9	36

Glossary

accrual accounting: A system in which item costs are realized at billing and are included in the financial statements as they are earned or incurred rather than as they are actually received or paid out in cash.

cash budget: A forecasted summary of a firm's expected cash flow and expected cash and loan balances.

completed contract: A procedure for computing payments on a contract in which payment is rendered and, thus, revenue earned after the entire job is satisfactorily completed.

current liabilities: These are a company's financial obligations to its creditors, suppliers, tax authorities, and others. The amount is due within one year.

current ratio: A ratio that reflects the relationship between current assets and current liabilities. It is a simple way to assess liquidity. This ratio provides an indication of a business ability to meet its current liabilities.

Current ratio = total current assets
÷ total current liabilities

debt-to-equity ratio: A ratio that provides the measure of money owed to creditors in relation to the equity value of the company.

Debt-to-equity ratio = total liabilities
÷ total equity

depreciation: A decrease in the value of equipment from use and the passage of time. Depreciation on business equipment is generally deductible for tax purposes over a number of years.

fixed asset: A tangible long-term asset such as land, buildings, or machinery, held for use rather than for processing or resale.

gross margin: Pretax net sales minus cost of sales. Also referred to as gross income.

gross profit margin: Gross profit divided by total revenue.

interest expense: Money that is paid out in interest on loans.

liability: A financial obligation (or the cash outlay) that must be made at a specific time to satisfy the contractual terms of such an obligation.

limited liability corporation (LLC): A corporate structure in which the business is liable, as an entity, for any losses or obligations. But the business owners are not personally liable.

long-term liabilities: Debts owned by the business that must be repaid more than one year from the date of the balance sheet.

net income before taxes: Income after cost of sales, operating expenses, sales and marketing expenses, indirect construction expenses, non-deductible deductions, and allowances have been subtracted from gross total income.

operating expenses: Expenses associated with running the business. Listed as a category on the profit and loss statement.

owner's equity: The amount of money that owners have directly invested in the business from the prior year's profits.

partnership: A contract between two or more persons who agree to pool talent and money to share profits or losses.

percentage of completion: An accounting system for computing partial payments on a large contract wherein identifiable portions of the work may be satisfactorily completed, invoiced and paid before the entire project is completed and paid in full. It is the percentage of cost incurred, multiplied by the total sales price for each job. This method can also be sued for a single job to better predict actual gross profit at completion.

net profit margin: Net profit before taxes divided by sales for a given 12-month period, expressed as a percentage.

profit sharing: A compensation arrangement in which employees received additional pay or benefits when the company earned or increased profit.

regular (or C) corporation: This is a standard business corporation in which earnings are taxed at the entity profitability level, before dividends. It is referred to as a "C" corporation because it is taxed under subsection C of the IRS code.

return on assets: A measure of profitability that indicates how effective the business is at earning money from the total assets dedicated to the business.

ROA ratio = net profit ÷ total assets

return on equity: A measure of profitability that indicates how effective the business is at earning money from the owner's invested capital.

ROE ratio = net profit ÷ total equity

S corporations: A domestically owned corporation with no more than 75 owners who have elected to pay taxes under subchapter S of the IRS Code. An S Corporation is taxed like a partnership: it is exempt from the corporate income tax, but its owners pay income taxes on all of the firm's income, including owner's wages, bonuses, etc., even if some of the earnings are retained by the firm.

sole proprietorship: A sole proprietorship is an unincorporated business that is owned by one individual. The owner is personally liable for any business debts.

Survey Questionnaire

2019 Remodelers' Cost of Doing Business Survey

Please report on your **fiscal year 2018 operations** as soon as possible. Participants will receive a **FREE electronic copy** of the *Remodelers' Cost of Doing Business Study, 2020 Edition.*

I. FIRM'S PROFILE

1. Indicate your firm's main operation during fiscal year 2018 and write in the percentage of your business that operation represents.

	Main operation (Check ONE only)	Percent of Your Business
Residential remodeling/rehabilitation	☐	_____ %
Commercial remodeling/rehabilitation	☐	_____ %
Single-family home building	☐	_____ %
Multifamily home building	☐	_____ %
Other (specify):_____	☐	_____ %

2. If your firm's main operation is residential remodeling/rehabilitation, please indicate which of the following best describes your firm:

☐ General remodeler   ☐ Specialty contractor
☐ Design-Build remodeler   ☐ Repair & maintenance contractor

3. How many years has your firm been in the residential remodeling business? _____ year(s)

4. How many jobs in each of the following price ranges did your firm complete in 2018?

Under $5,000	_____	$25,000 to $99,999	_____
$5,000 to $24,999	_____	$100,000 or more	_____

5. On average, how many <u>full-time employees</u> (including yourself) did your firm have on payroll in 2018? (If you had part-time employees, please use full time equivalents, defined as number of paid hours in each job class divided by 2,080 hours)

Office _____   Field _____   Sales _____

II. FINANCIAL INFORMARTION

6. Balance Sheet

Each code number refers to the NAHB Chart of Accounts, Appendix D, found at www.nahb.org/chart			
Assets		**Liabilities and Owner's Equity**	
Cash [1000-1090]	$	**Current liabilities** [2000-2490]	$
Accounts and notes receivables [1200-1290]	$	**Long-term liabilities** [2500-2700]	$
Other current assets [1100-1190; 1300-1690]	$	**Owner's equity** [2900-2960]	$
Other assets [1700-1990]	$		
Total Assets*	$	**Total Liabilities and Owner's Equity***	$

- Total assets must equal the total of liabilities plus owner's equity.

7. Income Statement

*Each code number refers to the NAHB Chart of Accounts, Appendix D, found at www.nahb.org/chart

Revenue from Operations		
Residential remodeling and repairs [3130,3135,3137]	$	
Commercial remodeling and repairs [3133]	$	
New single-family home building [3100-3125]	$	
All other revenue [3000, 3050, 3140, 3150, 3160-3490]	$	
Total company revenue [sum of the previous four entries]		$
Cost of Sales		
Labor for residential remodeling/repairs (include fringe benefits) [3810-3820]	$	
Material for residential remodeling/repairs [3830]	$	
Trade contractors for residential remodeling/repairs [3840]	$	
Commercial remodeling and repairs direct construction costs [3633]	$	
New single-family direct construction costs [3600,3610,3620,3625] (permits, labor with burden, materials, trade contractors) and Land [3550]	$	
All other costs of sales (related to items that fall under "All other revenue")	$	
Total company cost of sales [sum of previous six entries]		$
Gross Profit		
Total Company Revenue less Total Company Cost of Sales		$
Operating Expenses		
Indirect construction costs [4000-4990] (Superintendents, vehicles, tools, warranty, construction equipment)	$	
Financing expenses [5000-5990] (points and interest on all business loans)	$	
Sales and Marketing expenses [6000-6990] (advertising, marketing, salaries and commissions to sales personnel)	$	
General and Administrative expenses [8000-8990] (salaries, payroll taxes and benefits, office expenses, vehicles, travel, entertainment, taxes, insurance, professional services, and depreciation) (exclude owner's compensation)	$	
Owner's compensation [8010] (owner's salary, draws, bonuses and benefits. Do Not include distributions from retained earnings)	$	
Total operating expenses [sum of previous five entries]		$
Net Income Before Taxes [total company gross profit minus total operating expenses]		$